Recipe

Your Hauntingly Delicious Recipe Title

Ingredients

Directions

Notes

Cookbook For The Recenttly Deceased

Recipe

Date:

Ingredients

Directions

Notes

Cookbook For The Recenttly Deceased

Recipe

Date:

Ingredients

Directions

Notes

Cookbook For The Recenttly Deceased

Recipe

Date:

Ingredients

Directions

Notes

Cookbook For The Recenttly Deceased

Recipe

Date:

Ingredients

Directions

Notes

Cookbook For The Recenttly Deceased

Recipe

Date:

Ingredients

Directions

Notes

Cookbook For The Recenttly Deceased

Recipe

Date:

Ingredients

Directions

Notes

Cookbook For The Recenttly Deceased

Recipe

Date:

Ingredients

Directions

Notes

Cookbook For The Recenttly Deceased

Recipe

Date:

Ingredients

Directions

Notes

Cookbook For The Recenttly Deceased

Recipe

Date:

Ingredients

Directions

Notes

Cookbook For The Recenttly Deceased

Recipe

Date:

Ingredients

Directions

Notes

Cookbook For The Recenttly Deceased

Recipe

Date:

Ingredients

Directions

Notes

Cookbook For The Recenttly Deceased

Recipe

Date:

Ingredients

Directions

Notes

Cookbook For The Recenttly Deceased

Recipe

Date:

Ingredients

Directions

Notes

Cookbook For The Recenttly Deceased

Recipe

Date:

Ingredients

Directions

Notes

Cookbook For The Recenttly Deceased

Recipe

Date:

Ingredients

Directions

Notes

Cookbook For The Recenttly Deceased

Recipe

Date:

Ingredients

Directions

Notes

Cookbook For The Recenttly Deceased

Recipe

Date:

Ingredients

Directions

Notes

Cookbook For The Recenttly Deceased

Recipe

Date:

Ingredients

Directions

Notes

Cookbook For The Recenttly Deceased

Recipe

Date:

Ingredients

Directions

Notes

Cookbook For The Recenttly Deceased

Recipe

Date:

Ingredients

Directions

Notes

Cookbook For The Recenttly Deceased

Recipe

Date:

Ingredients

Directions

Notes

Cookbook For The Recenttly Deceased

Recipe

Date:

Ingredients

Directions

Notes

Cookbook For The Recenttly Deceased

Recipe

Date:

Ingredients

Directions

Notes

Cookbook For The Recenttly Deceased

Recipe

Date:

Ingredients

Directions

Notes

Cookbook For The Recenttly Deceased

Recipe

Date:

Ingredients

Directions

Notes

Cookbook For The Recenttly Deceased

Recipe

Date:

Ingredients

Directions

Notes

Cookbook For The Recenttly Deceased

Recipe

Date:

Ingredients

Directions

Notes

Cookbook For The Recenttly Deceased

Recipe

Date:

Ingredients

Directions

Notes

Cookbook For The Recenttly Deceased

Recipe

Date:

Ingredients

Directions

Notes

Cookbook For The Recenttly Deceased

Recipe

Date:

Ingredients

Directions

Notes

Cookbook For The Recenttly Deceased

Recipe

Date:

Ingredients

Directions

Notes

Cookbook For The Recenttly Deceased

Recipe

Date:

Ingredients

Directions

Notes

Cookbook For The Recenttly Deceased

Recipe

Date:

Ingredients

Directions

Notes

Cookbook For The Recenttly Deceased

Recipe

Date:

Ingredients

Directions

Notes

Cookbook For The Recenttly Deceased

Recipe

Date:

Ingredients

Directions

Notes

Cookbook For The Recenttly Deceased

Recipe

Date:

Ingredients

Directions

Notes

Cookbook For The Recenttly Deceased

Recipe

Date:

Ingredients

Directions

Notes

Cookbook For The Recenttly Deceased

Recipe

Date:

Ingredients

Directions

Notes

Cookbook For The Recenttly Deceased

Recipe

Date:

Ingredients

Directions

Notes

Cookbook For The Recenttly Deceased

Recipe

Date:

Ingredients

Directions

Notes

Cookbook For The Recenttly Deceased

Recipe

Date:

Ingredients

Directions

Notes

Cookbook For The Recenttly Deceased

Recipe

Date:

Ingredients

Directions

Notes

Cookbook For The Recenttly Deceased

Recipe

Date:

Ingredients

Directions

Notes

Cookbook For The Recenttly Deceased

Recipe

Date:

Ingredients

Directions

Notes

Cookbook For The Recenttly Deceased

Recipe

Date:

Ingredients

Directions

Notes

Cookbook For The Recenttly Deceased

Recipe

Date:

Ingredients

Directions

Notes

Cookbook For The Recenttly Deceased

Recipe

Date:

Ingredients

Directions

Notes

Cookbook For The Recenttly Deceased

Recipe

Date:

Ingredients

Directions

Notes

Cookbook For The Recenttly Deceased

Recipe

Date:

Ingredients

Directions

Notes

Cookbook For The Recenttly Deceased

Recipe

Date:

Ingredients

Directions

Notes

Cookbook For The Recenttly Deceased

Recipe

Date:

Ingredients

Directions

Notes

Cookbook For The Recenttly Deceased

Recipe

Date:

Ingredients

Directions

Notes

Cookbook For The Recenttly Deceased

Recipe

Date:

Ingredients

Directions

Notes

Cookbook For The Recenttly Deceased

Recipe

Date:

Ingredients

Directions

Notes

Cookbook For The Recenttly Deceased

Recipe

Date:

Ingredients

Directions

Notes

Cookbook For The Recenttly Deceased

Recipe

Date:

Ingredients

Directions

Notes

Cookbook For The Recenttly Deceased

Recipe

Date:

Ingredients

Directions

Notes

Cookbook For The Recenttly Deceased

Recipe

Date:

Ingredients

Directions

Notes

Cookbook For The Recenttly Deceased

Recipe

Date:

Ingredients

Directions

Notes

Cookbook For The Recenttly Deceased

Recipe

Date:

Ingredients

Directions

Notes

Cookbook For The Recenttly Deceased

Recipe

Date:

Ingredients

Directions

Notes

Cookbook For The Recenttly Deceased

Recipe

Date:

Ingredients

Directions

Notes

Cookbook For The Recenttly Deceased

Recipe

Date:

Ingredients

Directions

Notes

Cookbook For The Recenttly Deceased

Recipe

Date:

Ingredients

Directions

Notes

Cookbook For The Recenttly Deceased

Recipe

Date:

Ingredients

Directions

Notes

Cookbook For The Recenttly Deceased

Recipe

Date:

Ingredients

Directions

Notes

Cookbook For The Recenttly Deceased

Recipe

Date:

Ingredients

Directions

Notes

Cookbook For The Recenttly Deceased

Recipe

Date:

Ingredients

Directions

Notes

Cookbook For The Recenttly Deceased

Recipe

Date:

Ingredients

Directions

Notes

Cookbook For The Recenttly Deceased

Recipe

Date:

Ingredients

Directions

Notes

Cookbook For The Recenttly Deceased

Recipe

Date:

Ingredients

Directions

Notes

Cookbook For The Recenttly Deceased

Recipe

Date:

Ingredients

Directions

Notes

Cookbook For The Recenttly Deceased

Recipe

Date:

Ingredients

Directions

Notes

Cookbook For The Recenttly Deceased

Recipe

Date:

Ingredients

Directions

Notes

Cookbook For The Recenttly Deceased

Recipe

Date:

Ingredients

Directions

Notes

Cookbook For The Recenttly Deceased

Recipe

Date:

Ingredients

Directions

Notes

Cookbook For The Recenttly Deceased

Recipe

Date:

Ingredients

Directions

Notes

Cookbook For The Recenttly Deceased

Recipe

Date:

Ingredients

Directions

Notes

Cookbook For The Recenttly Deceased

Recipe

Date:

Ingredients

Directions

Notes

Cookbook For The Recenttly Deceased

Recipe

Date:

Ingredients

Directions

Notes

Cookbook For The Recenttly Deceased

Recipe

Date:

Ingredients

Directions

Notes

Cookbook For The Recenttly Deceased

Recipe

Date:

Ingredients

Directions

Notes

Cookbook For The Recenttly Deceased

Recipe

Date:

Ingredients

Directions

Notes

Cookbook For The Recenttly Deceased

Recipe

Date:

Ingredients

Directions

Notes

Cookbook For The Recenttly Deceased

Recipe

Date:

Ingredients

Directions

Notes

Cookbook For The Recenttly Deceased

Recipe

Date:

Ingredients

Directions

Notes

Cookbook For The Recenttly Deceased

Recipe

Date:

Ingredients

Directions

Notes

Cookbook For The Recenttly Deceased

Recipe

Date:

Ingredients

Directions

Notes

Cookbook For The Recenttly Deceased

Recipe

Date:

Ingredients

Directions

Notes

Cookbook For The Recenttly Deceased

Recipe

Date:

Ingredients

Directions

Notes

Cookbook For The Recenttly Deceased

Recipe

Date:

Ingredients

Directions

Notes

Cookbook For The Recenttly Deceased

Recipe

Date:

Ingredients

Directions

Notes

Cookbook For The Recenttly Deceased

Recipe

Date:

Ingredients

Directions

Notes

Cookbook For The Recenttly Deceased

Recipe

Date:

Ingredients
Directions
Notes

Cookbook For The Recenttly Deceased

Recipe

Date:

Ingredients

Directions

Notes

Cookbook For The Recenttly Deceased

Recipe

Date:

Ingredients

Directions

Notes

Cookbook For The Recenttly Deceased

Recipe

Date:

Ingredients

Directions

Notes

Cookbook For The Recenttly Deceased

Recipe

Date:

Ingredients

Directions

Notes

Cookbook For The Recenttly Deceased

CPSIA information can be obtained
at www.ICGtesting.com
Printed in the USA
BVHW011307111121
621377BV00011B/251